# Wacky Doodles

## COLORING BOOK FOR GROWN-UPS

*Majestic* **COLORING**

ISBN: 978-1517557805

# FREE DOWNLOAD

## 12 FUN DESIGNS FOR YOUR COLORING ENJOYMENT!

**This 'n That Coloring Book for Grown-Ups** is bundled up in one convenient PDF file to download and print at your leisure.

Sign up for our Majestic Coloring mailing list and get a free copy of **This 'n That Coloring Book for Grown-Ups**.

Click here to get started
http://majesticcoloring.com/thisnthat-free